Cinder

ALSO BY BRUCE BOND

Books

THE THROATS OF NARCISSUS
RADIOGRAPHY
THE ANTEROOM OF PARADISE
INDEPENDENCE DAYS

Chapbooks

NATIONAL BLOOD
THE POSSIBLE
BROKEN CIRCLE
THE IVORY HOURS

Cinder

BRUCE BOND

etruscan press

Etruscan Press
P.O. Box 9685
Silver Spring, MD 20916-9685

www.etruscanpress.org

1 2 3 4 5 6 7 8 9 0

Publisher's Cataloging-in-Publication
  (Provided by Quality Books, Inc.)

Bond, Bruce, 1954-
    Cinder / by Bruce Bond. -- 1st ed.
    p.cm.
    ISBN 0-9718228-5-9

    I. Title.

PS3552.O5943C56 2003   811'.54
                                 QBI33-1019

for George and Winifred Bond

and for Nicki
my awakening, my ash

Acknowledgments

Artful Dodge	Black Sun
	River
Beloit Poetry Journal	Vigil
Black Warrior Review	Rope
Colorado Review	Dementia Praecox
	Rebirth
COLUMBIA: A Journal of Literature and Art	Heaven
Crab Orchard Review	Palimpsest
Denver Quarterly	Chants
	Monument for Leone Vivante
Descant	Joy
Epoch	Cortege
Harvard Review	The Altars of September
Image: A Journal of the Arts and Religion	Babel
Nimrod	Litany
	Polyphony
The Ohio Review	Passacaglia
The Paris Review	The Eyes of Odilon Redon
	The Island City of Dmitri Shostakovich
	The Lovers of Rome
Passages North	Descendant
	Monument
	Pilgrim
Ploughshares	Testament
River Styx	The Fall
	Terminal
The Sewanee Review	Uroborus
Shenandoah	The General's Leg
The Southeast Review	A Flock of Phantom Limbs Gathers at the Border

"Uroborus" appeared as "Circular Breathing" in *E: The Emily Dickinson Award Anthology* (University West Press). "The Altars of September" appeared in *September 11, 2001: American Writers Respond* (Etruscan Press). "The Fall" won a River Styx International Poetry Award. "A Flock of Phantom Limbs Gathers at the Border" won the Gearhart Poetry Prize; in addition it appeared in *American Diaspora: Poetry of Displacement* (University of Iowa Press). "Passacaglia" appeared in the chapbook *The Possible* (Gerald Cable Prize, Silverfish Review Press). The author would like to thank the National Endowment for the Arts, the University of North Texas, and the Texas Commission on the Arts for their financial assistance. Also a special thanks to Nicki Cohen, Chad Davidson, Austin Hummell, Corey Marks, Donald Revell, and Matthew Roth for their wisdom and kindness during the completion of this manuscript.

Contents

I.

RIVER

If you dip your hand in,
your wrist would ache immediately,
your bones would begin to ache and your hand burn
as if the water were a transmutation of fire
that feeds on stones and burns with a dark gray flame.

—ELIZABETH BISHOP

Cortege

Those famished hours a square of sunlight
gradually passes its untouched plate,
when the afternoon cola fizzes like a fuse,
the doused beds of headstones smoking,

when huddled in chains newspaper cages
stand empty on the seafloor of Texas
in August, the courthouse sidewalk fresh-
swept in field-dust and the longest days;

or under migrant shadows, when you watch
cars glide like hot tar, headlights burning,
tunneling the summer glare, the black of day;
you would swear you've been here before

if only for the prayer of saying so
in a blistered place resembling nowhere,
here where the slate-colored cargo of grief
squeals its shipyard cables and descends,

your heart a dock of strangers staring.
You know them all: the ash trees stripped
to nervous systems breezes run through,
harbor gulls from Corpus Christi who turn

their rusted wheel of flight; already waters
drag the fine serrations of their shells,
already the fragrance of funeral
parlors in your hair. And you shine blackly

under mirages midday makes—we all do,
breathing underwater, hoisting our limbs,
a coffin afloat in the palms we curl,
the brass like sun we grip to still it.

Polyphony

The song of the siskin clips
a tiny eyelet in the morning quiet—never
the same sweet notes, though nearly,
ever the wily reed startling its throat.
Whatever the need blistered there made new
with every variation, however small its source,
it calls out from an enormous distance,
like a grave we fly to, tended by strangers,
opening a narrow channel of grief.

My wife gazes at the minted plaque
they lay her father under, the newly
starved and spotted hands silent
as a surgeon's, crossed at the breathless
chest of a man that no one ever knew.
Or so we wondered. Those final nights
his heart's fist pounded for release.
Another day, another spat of babble and fire,
another word stumbling out like teeth.

All those years he laid displays at the table,
the dire affection and rabbinical prayers,
those blessings he raised like tall knives
to open the steaming sides of birds,
who could have glimpsed it coming, that spit
he swallowed, the ancient fluster, dry sobs,
rage at the woman he loved so hard, so long?
To see him blush with the surfacing fury,
his throated veins stiffening like stems,

who wouldn't marvel at the awful grace
of survival—so tough to watch, tough
to look away—the blind eye
of the livid will? One moment
morning's icy dazzle locked him in a trance—
there's time when any luster stings—
and then the deeper strangeness,
a whispered music, wild and tuneless,
scattering syllables, moving his lips.

That's what it is to live in a world
stretched by the hands of birth and death;
there's music everywhere you leave it.
My wife sings a muted Kaddish
to remember his voice, to give it a branch
to perch on, feel the breathing
chambers in him dwindle and swell.
The foreign tongue is an odd bird
flitting in its shelter, a hope-sick messenger

passing through. I read along in translation—
Blessed is He, who is beyond all blessings—
and think how it might have ruffled
and teased him: the ceremonial sweep
that finalizes nothing. Phrase after phrase
her singing clouds against the chill.
It shines the air, like any song worth singing
twice, or, as we say, we sing *by heart*,
each seed in us poised to break its skin.

These are the days the sun aches
to go forward and back at the same time,
when, like music, we long to be refreshed
by silence, laid bare to the ravenous
mercies of the season. My wife's prayer,
verse by verse, would smother his casket
in its seedlings, the flowered earth below
surprised by dawn, his rage released,
the sound of birdsong ripping up the sky.

Rope

Who was it who first believed
each strand of our experience
is coiled into the long ropes
of the brain, that no matter
how many dawns break their waves
of light over the eye, we manage
to hoard it, all of it, and if
only we could wire some charge
into the right place, we are there,
born across the frightened
sheets of a mother's blood,
entire, having broken the water
of our denial, without the current
sweetness of memory and loss;
and to test our faith, we will live
our whole lives over, and burn
both ends of this fuse to the center,
remembering and not remembering,
and bearing in mind the difference,
and not bearing, until we come
to the moment the wire dreams
its own descent, that little
charge of pure illusion,
and its laying down of ropes—
who can blame us after all—
in the phantom ropes we are, we are.

Uroborus

To see the cobra's green gold rise
from its basket, those frightened eyes
pinned to the measly lizard inside
its hood, pharaoh-bright, sanctified,
glittering in scales of armor,
who's to say who's the charmer,
who's the charmed, what it is that binds
each body to the other's mind?

Who could listen to the long strand
of music passing through those hands
unbroken and not feel a bit
deceived, to think his wind could slip
into a circle outward and back
as if his breathing were a snake
swallowing its own tail? A trick,
true, how he floats the reedy brook

of air, inhaling as he blows,
cheeks puffed like an organ bellow.
It draws the snake however deaf
just so close, no closer, adrift
in a shadow-charm of the charm,
the serpentine *s* a wind chime
where it wavers brushed by the oboe's
shyest movement. What the cobra

senses, God knows. Still it's human
to pick at the lock of heaven,
that look of rapture's river-mill
spilling over, cell after cell
of the wheel weighted to the brim
and falling, the sheer momentum
like a stillness in the bloodstream,
each cycle consuming, consumed.

We who listen in the Bombay sun—
tourists mostly, local children—
some of us are lost to our own
mantra, our own black column of wind.
Not that the hazard alone is
charm enough, but how some silence,
some core of creature solitude
there, keeps dying into a tune

we love, like a corpse trimmed in blooms
and candles, in life's asylum.
Sunlight slowly trails its bright ash
above us. Nearby, a midday flash
and honk of cabs, the occasional
fruit truck eager for arrival.
What song could travel far here, save
the one we take up as we leave

our petty cash? How it tempts us,
to see the soul as karma's tourist
fearful and enamored, a fresh
dread returning, flesh after flesh.
No end to the strange flirtation
we feel, watering a tongue
in music: with every sweet sting
of the reed, a poison rising.

River

While we never step in the same stream twice,
　　　　the same story as we know it,
　　　　　　　the same dark room we wake and rise to,

so too there's a river we never leave,
　　　　which is why, as I checked my watch that morning
　　　　　　　before we drove to put our cat to sleep,

I felt a heavy current at the backs
　　　　of my knees, an invisible water
　　　　　　　on my arms, my chest, over my head,

and at the bottom of it all our cat,
　　　　oblivious, walking a crooked line,
　　　　　　　attending to her ritual of meat and pills.

How deceitful we felt as we carried her
　　　　trusting body newly groomed, laid it out
　　　　　　　on the steel table, committing ourselves

to the final motions: the humming shaver
　　　　over her leg, the needle's slow insertion,
　　　　　　　a bead of blood in the gradual syringe,

and her eyes, now milky with age,
　　　　sealing up as her neck wilted, death's
　　　　　　　white blossom in my unfamiliar hand.

It's as if some shine lay buried
　　　　in the details, in the cold tray
　　　　　　　of sterile silver, the bright cloth

and gloved assurance so vivid inside
     the shy confusion of our mercy.
          Such power in a final day it seems

an overdose of life, a flooding
     of the open eye. No wisdom
          could prepare us for the prick and wonder,

how her gaze would narrow as if in pleasure,
     the way I half-expected to feel her ghost
          flitting through me, though I never did,

the body released, we say, though oddly weighted,
     like a mirror the night had fallen
          into, cleared of its last ripple of breath.

Descendant

Who could be lured away from the lion
with the freshly slit head of a kudu
in her paws, its cropped throat hemmed in laces
of meat, the spires of its horns recoiling
as if in the wind of a great surprise.

The way she grooms the kudu's curling fur
you would think it was a drowsy child
warm and pliant, what she leaves her life to,
under the soft abrasions of her tongue
the lazy eyelids opening and closing.

A cub tugs at the teats of shredded gut
and drinks there; with every nod he makes,
the savor of one blood meets another,
briny and strange as the sea must be
where it ravishes an estuary current.

And all around them the tattered reeds
flutter and moan, as mother and cub
also moan, until their stomachs sag
like sacks of milk and sleep defeats them,
the suns of their heads lowered to the ground,

until the whole scene resolves to a sizzle
of flies, that and the careless twitch you see
in sleeping things, as if the kudu were still
breathing in their minds, still shuddering
with the last sensations of its legs.

The fresher the slaughter the greater the thrill
trickling from the earth: grain by grain
the busy pincers of the weaver ants
dismantle an edge of the kudu's eye,
veins of them piercing the softest tissue

as if to harvest the light that's stored there.
They are sparks in some rapacious fire
glittering as it eats, some meditation
moving without horror or regret,
sinking deep into the body's creases.

A bead ascends the tunnel of the ear.
Such work has something brazen in it, quick,
meticulous, watchful as a blind man's hand
over a sacred script. Beneath the windbreak
of the vanishing face, a distant roar.

Dementia Praecox

Not the adequate darling of the literal heart,
the turned backs of doorways and chairs
choosing themselves in stillness, not the wind

that scrawls its gossip through the trees,
the pollen of their wilding tongues, but more:
more a rage for law, for the interlocking

of parts; spite the parts, says the law,
spite the law, spite the acetylene dusk
that refuses to weld, mother to child,

the canopy of rusted stems that chafe
the arbor into the law, spite the water
which would still the fire that melts

a world to water, spite the face, the stone-
white smeared in a father's silence,
sheer swallowing mirror-rivers of silence,

spite the severed hand where it wanders,
it knows nothing of its crime against
the law, voices cast their hooks

over the public garden, spite the mockery
of birds who take their song to the thrushes,
to the frozen spittle of the faucets,

the dread that begat the weather that begat
the thick coats and wide brims of the impeccable
and smug, the law demands they are smug

and remain so in their powerful joy
and tossed hair, their wretched accomplishment,
spite the crust that boils into hills

over the back of the world, this ground
in an oiled mesh of worms, conspiring,
rage for the tiny sirens of their gears,

for the optic fiber, slithering, lit,
its prick of searchlight on a veinal
puzzle, there where the palpitations begin:

everything, everything: every morning

vertical blood mushrooms into lobes, weapon
to end all weapons, rage for romance,
the clawed latch on a heart-shaped box,

for the pulse of the echo to woo
the echo, to feel it flutter in its own
teeth like a fist you bite for comfort.

Vigil

Nights I take my lost sleep to the one lamp
    left burning in this house and thoughts of the man

hospiced in a room next door, when, not knowing
    where to turn, I am hanging on by a thread of music,

the last stitch closing a heart in its shroud.
    Just what binds me at the other end is unclear,

though slowly as my hands work the frets, they take on
    their life, like pigeons in a magician's vase—

which is part of the thread's resilience, grazing
    the tiny hairs of the ear, part of why, having come

so far, I hesitate now to snip it with sleep.
    It simply melts, the way the green line melts

in a heart monitor, slicing through its box
    and melting, though I like to think it follows

something, that my neighbor where he lies, slack-jawed,
    stunned with damage, offers up the needle

of a kindred music; for his curtain is no less
    troubled with lamplight, and as his pulse flits

about in its cage, the same thread of air goes
    through him, holding nothing going in, nothing going out.

The Fall

I.

We have come this way before,
my father's body laid out like one horizon
we cannot cross, gone soft with all
the suns it swallowed.

I am stepping into a paper boat.

What is it that leaves in pieces. Cleansed.

We wake, my father and I,
in the middle of my sleep.
Where there is no sleep, there is nothing but.

This ground, this cloud, calling.

II.

Day eight and he surfaces faintly,
his eye opening now and then
with its portal to the mind's dark,
the enormous wilderness, listening,
sending out an invisible tremor.

It thrills us like the sighting
of a whale breaking daylight.
Never have I felt so close to the shine,
so drawn to the living circle,
laid bare to the quiet claim it makes.

I'm at a loss now what to tell him,
my words repeating as if they dissolved
at once, each sound set down
in the water of his silence.
I hear the talk of other rooms.

In time we are indistinguishable
from what we cannot say.
It binds one life to the next,
this patch of white falling into white.
The respirator crests and surges.

We hold that sensation just long enough
for his eye to glaze,
the mighty fish in him drawing air
and diving, bearing light
to the starless reaches below.

III.

In my closet waits a black coat
dark as a path under ocean air
through the middle of the night.

Sky salts the body where it wanders.

IV.

There is a day beside a river
in Idlewild, California
where my father laid a hand
over a bump I got, a head welt
he christened *little goose egg*,
and I ached a while, stunned,
though not without a shadow of pride.

After all I was with child now,
the compress of his palm turning
then to the trace of a palm,
a phantom crown from the man
who seemed to me a founding
father of the world,
a child's world, granted,

though even now as he falters
on the brink of something vaster,
I see the day simmer
like pavement doused in gasoline.
It dazes me still, this shine
of blood inside me, as if to bruise
myself were to polish something

older than the names we carry.
If only I could lay my palm
over the eye of his wound
as if to blind it, to take its power away.
Anything to answer this
constant swelling, to leave there
a phantom hand, still as ice.

V.

Tear down the curtains
and the fever of day upon them.
Tear down the scrim of sky
with its ragged hole of sunlight.
Tear down the sun, a shock
of stars scattering in its wake.
Tear down the night's fabric,
the cruelty of loss and behind it
the terrible charity of greater loss.
Tear down the pole star

and let the others come undone
sparkling like bees.
Tear open a place for the moon
to rise, for the fist,
the skull, the flower of it.
Tear out the image of the moon
in our eyes and give it back.
Give it all back, the field
of broken teeth, the bees,
the hungry patterns they make.
Make an offering of molecules,
of the pinched stars
that are our bodies.
Make a beacon of this heap
of scraps and fire.
Let us beat the black door of the sky
and deliver what we've made,
what we've torn, this minor mountain
of horror and seed, this compost
of worlds, this father,
this welter, this sting, this son.

VI.

When I sleep I wear my father's face,
his blind amazement, the zero
of his open mouth. I am calling out
after him, the way one calls
to a taxi deafened by rain.

The weary, the damned, the smitten,
the deceived, the prayer unanswered,
the long lines of their descent,
in each a little earth, returning.
The pulse, the pride, the mercury, the snow.

In my chest I carry him fallen there.
To breathe hard is to hear
the shush and tumble—I do—
the sound of air erasing itself,
a car radio entering a tunnel.

Rebirth

What is it in the dark dawn of rain
that coaxes sleep from its cranial cove?

Veins of rivulets grapple
the window glass, longing for admittance.

What is it in the softening panels
of your roof, in the widow veil of starlight

under no star, the burrowing body
in its bedsheets, the burrowing heart in its chest?

Could it be a steadiness comes over us
in the midst of all that coming apart,

the sound of prayer beads worried from their circle?
Never have you felt so cradled

in the luster of your mooring,
so narrow in the slip that rocks you blind.

Could it be the tiny stemware
of a million nameless christenings?

Your house leans its prow behind you—
you who give in to your appetite, who hear

in the rain the leafy crackle of a long
awaited approach—the Lord giveth,

the Lord stealeth away—so long you wait
you take it for departure.

II.

Monument

When the fire devours itself, when the power turns against itself, it seems as if the whole being is made complete at the instant of its final ruin and that the intensity of the destruction is the supreme proof, the clearest proof, of its existence.   —Gaston Bachelard

Chants

Once through the ear's auricle
before you reach the acoustic meatus, you find
the *pinna*, the feather, the wing,
from which we get *pen* and *appetite*, the stylus
working a membranous page,
its vigilant shivers pin-tipped, penned
with the yearning of a hermit
in his wax-lit carrel.
Picture St. Gregory,
a dove on his shoulder whispering
the stuff of chant that bears his name.
Never was the world so immediate, so strange.

Be still, it coos, *close your eyes, listen*
through the hunger in the mouth of the labyrinth,
through the tiny chafe of the wing
scratching at the door for corporeal sky.
Picture the man doing his best
bird imitation, his head tucked
into his body, humpbacked, fidgety, small.
He wets his pen in the inkwell's pupil,
under beady eyes a psalmistry of neumes
perched in cages, awaiting flight.
So slight the span between terror and song.

His pen looks up having blackened
many a parchment since the last plague,
when looking on was near contagion.
What repulsed the eye the ear would better receive.
A mercy, how we turn a bit to listen closer.
Spiritus, sings the dove, *spiritus mundi*,
though the man knows in light
of a certain weightlessness he feels
a bird speaks in speechless embers.
So it is with the music of the spheres,
what he cannot hear because
he always hears it. Never so immediate, so strange.

If the ear has but one page
drinking its inscriptions, no matter.
Between the tremble of the thunderhead
and the sleep it shakes: a little appetite;
between the thrum of the arrow and the deer's
    shimmering pulse,
in the tiny toolshed of bones that can never be mended,
between the lover's reticence and the reticence
it enters, the one it receives, between the teeth
of the real and the tongue of the imagined,
between the cochlea's lips filigreed with vanishings,
between the between and the polar caps,
be they holy or human,
those papery regions without commerce of birds,
without ink, without a living itch to scratch.

The Altars of September

That night she closed her eyes and saw
the trapped birds of voices shatter
against the crumbling walls, like a scene
in a movie replaying the disaster,
lighting up the back of the brain.
With each collapse the glass rose up,
restored, bright with sky, the fist
of God a shadow-plane approaching.

And it felt so distant, the numb
comfort that would bear this image
into the first cold regions of sleep,
the blackboard of the body wet
and remless, as if those towers
fell still deeper through the floor
of the mind, gone the way of the pill
she took in faith, swallowing the world.

However many nights she clicked
her TV off, its spark of light
dwindling into the clear stone,
it would take time for any shape
slipping through her hands to lie
down in clay or paper, any lip
of paint to redden her brush.
White was its own confession.

She always imagined the distance
between a painting of a day
and the day behind it as a path
that carries us into our lives,
giving us more room, more reason
to move, luring us on and in
like sleep so deep in the body
all we see is of the body.

In time, looking out this way
through the window of her canvas,
every cloud dragging its anchor
becomes a burden of the flesh,
not hers alone, but the stuff
of what no solitary gaze
can tear there from heaven's fire,
what no frame can ever shelter.

Just that morning before she heard
the news, she took the shore drive south,
set up her easel, all the while
an unaccountable strangeness
drawn down over the folding cliffs,
a stillness unlike any day,
the uneasy silence of the skies
that hour tender as an eye.

Palimpsest

In the film *Hiroshima*, with each bloom
on our horizon a subtitled English

pales under the blanch of light, infused,
so what you hear, the musical blur

of the foreign tongue, suddenly floats
its story above the burning planet,

over the heads of most spectators here,
lost to a white shock, if only briefly,

then the script emerges blazing its way
out of the underworld, bearing cinders.

And it keeps happening, blast after blast
bannered in music, each word an Orpheus

descending into the burial flash,
a lantern blinded in the open flame.

There is nothing that it turns away,
this light, no lock so small it would not pick it,

the cloud's brainstem swelling in the mind.
You would think the brilliant arm of God

broke out of the earth's core, like a man
drowning in solid ground, his voice gone under.

There are nights so still they are breakable
as glass. As silence. A body knows this.

A body knows and moves beneath its knowing.
The credits rise. We wake our distant feet.

And as we leave under the iron-red trees,
our mouths so much colder now, breathing

smoke, as the first ice begins to sparkle,
we walk the stone theater stairs in clusters,

reluctant down the stunned October path.

Monument for Leone Vivante

And then the moment you just passed through
pools in your wake, its whorled glass fused
with anonymous light, the possible flash
of lust, or panic, a glad spark scribbling
its equation. Or was it your face,

the agate of each iris filmed in water,
your hair blown back by the lens, singed white,
so now you ghost a world, just beyond
the solvent mirror, to fog a table rusting
on its porch, flecked in daylight, above it

a shiny olive grove of eyes awakened
into stillness. That's when the beloved
window goes clear, when the fiery rectangle
plunges back into a shatter of leaves.
Sun burns a bottomless hole in the sky.

Indivisible, you said, the blue
we come from, as if with every momentary
death, each disbelief in a stand of trees,
our hands are homing pigeons passing through
the glass. How better to rehearse a past

that never comes, to close ourselves in that
particular grave, if only to test
the potency of our failures, how words
spirit out of their bodies, estranged,
a face in the constant freshness of the dark.

Testament

Almost winter and the groundskeepers are firing
        blanks into the trees,
scattering a nuisance of grackles from the branches—
        enough, say the guns,
of excrement and birdsong, and the sudden sight

is futility: great fistfuls
        of black confetti, the way they soar out shrill
with panic and return
        as if history would take them back, blowing
its leaves onto the trees again.

And with each return a storm of words falls
        into the limbs' antennae.
They are drawn into a woman's story,
        a woman's voice,
in her throat a nervous gathering of wings.

She was a nun, flightless in her robe and habit,
        pale under the scorch
and stare of a foreign sun, of a day men bound
        her eyes in burlap,
led her through a hole in the quiet planet.

For every profanity they put
        her through—these men who keep revisiting
her sleep—she feels profane
        to speak it, to go down that trail of burns
to the core of the disaster.

Which is more than any act at the center,
          the torturous
logic of pliers and knives, more than the open
          mouths of wounds
welling up with unspeakable life.

Beneath the scavenging aftermath of birds
          feasting,
she knows a silence that is a parody of mercy.
          It bears a head
without a face, an inability to forgive.

She opens her mouth and birds fly out.
          They are a flock of hooks
in the sky's fabric. To remember is to be wholly herself.
          Almost dark. She opens her mouth
and the trees inhale.

A Flock of Phantom Limbs Gathers
at the Border

An amputee is a brood of indecisions.
The scent of smoke lingers in her shirt.

Refugees crowd the bare plain passing the secrets
of their diseases, on their backs the iron rain clouds melding.

A child scours a rock with her gaze
as if to eradicate the face she sees there.

They keep coming to this place, faces
uneasy as cities flowing into cities, where linen tents

flap their bloodless wings, where sleep
endangers, where the silence of the exhausted

is the dropped jaw of a sanctuary wall.
Behind them an army of scribes and bits of char

write one history over another. A holy city
is an insomniac book: black page, black page.

A man is entering an alien airspace, a cold front
of bodies moving over the face of the earth.

He carries his language like a bag
of bread and disinfectant. He is not quite

in this nation he's in, but he's close,
approaching the great collapse when sky groans

like a long-locked gear and the thunderhead
opens its thick fist. He does not stop walking

where he lies, flecked in sores and the first few drops.
He does not roll into the palm of the state.

He hears the thrum of planes like some immense stone
bearing down through a hole in the world.

Monument

When the news came it took silence to make room:
the great ice block of knowledge warped
the floor, the blood sluggish
to give our hands back. Water dropped
its veils over windows and sizzled.

When the news came we rolled out of beds
into mirrors fixed at the backs of our lives.
Gauges in airplanes locked up crackling
into radio static; trumpet-colored ropes
lowered their miniature casket in our ears

and the first spade of dirt rolled its drum.
When the news came we forgot everything
even the news. Bronze words scorched the air.
Each cold kindness trembled in its star.
Knowing less than before was a house

glassed in winter, and at the center of the house
the tiny scraps of newsprint, burning.
When the news came a swoon of sparks polished our eyes.
We heard the chimes of milk in refrigerators
at midnight, the monuments lit with disbelief.

The General's Leg

In memory of Dan Sickles, Union General

He was thinking about the severed leg
again, and why not? It was still his
after all, still withering under glass
in a small museum. Who else would drag
a butchered life this far, to stand so

long for so little, one-legged as a flag,
over the infant casket where it lay,
flesh of his flesh, preserved, though sadly,
its dry skin fastening about the bone,
and him there staring it down as if blown

backward out of his own body, stiff
and winded, a thin cane in either hand.
However faithful the half that slaved
beneath him, perspiring in its dark sleeve,
he doted on the part that tore away.

It became his every next step, his ticket,
his ugly habit, a kind of memorial
path chilled and paling in the gaslight.
All those nights it seemed to leave him,
sliding between the legs of women,

or thrashing in his sleep like a boy
treading water. And now, to see it float
in the red felt, long after the phantom
leg flickered out between them, as if
this is what it is to walk out of a life

and look back, the gore of it nearly
believable now, its lurid carpentry
of medics with saws, the soiled hems of tents,
candles shuddering on their bayonets.
Let alone the arms where they shivered

in a pile of arms, their live fingers
tugged like puppets; it's what a stray limb
does in the end, for a time at least,
how the gases flutter out like bits of ghost.
That's why he came, to rise a little,

proud, damaged, hobbling up the marble stair,
or braced in the ancient elevator.
It was part of his body now, the wooden rail
and feel, the pale box rising, teetering
over the black shaft, a column of air.

Litany

A boy slips his foot into the mouth
of a shoe and gazes at his mother.
Shoe, she answers, pouting as though

the word hung on as a bloom of air.
She threads a lace through its eyelet,
pulls, repeats. And he lights up,

to see his leg disappearing there,
smooth and fleshy in the astonished jaw,
his body a great warm cloud of shoe-breath.

Then he teeters to his feet and walks
into the solitude of mere things.
Irrepressible, these things, how one day

they just seem to burst like stones
from the silent ground: the spoon, the bug,
the crayon melting in a slash of sunlight.

He throws his voice into their meager throats.
Remember me, they say. And the dizzy
ghost of *spoon* flutters up, redeemed.

Soon the air is an upward drizzle
of names, each rushing out of its body
into his. And it's almost charity,

his hunger, how he suffers the world
to come unto him. *Shoe, bug, mother.*
There is nothing he would not put his lips to.

Babel

A child's delight: the topple of any towering thing,
let alone one so storied, so intricately bricked
and trimmed as this, our Palace Hotel, diva
of its era, this flagship from our founding years.

It makes a person gape a little, eyes heavenward,
cameras cocked for the thump and rumble,
that greedy bloom of dust swallowing its monster
so that this moment becomes a thing

of beauty, a thrill to spite our lingering remorse.
I like to think the fall at Babel was no less
sublime, a blessing for its people's efforts,
vain as they were, foolish with their human share.

So ripe they'd grown with a child's pride, yes,
but so it should be with the childish among us,
piling spires in the sand, lording over cities
voiced with the stuff of heaven's mother tongue.

The offense we give is how we grow into solitude,
our unsteady selves lifted to the floor of heaven
until the heart's collapse is less a shattering
of one language than the breakdown of a dream,

and a troubled dream at that, the way it looms
like a stern premise of belonging, how it presupposes
some singular mouth in the plaza of our lives,
some fountain we cast our silver into, all of us

under one shadowy flag lashing at its halyards.
This said, it wasn't the hand of indignation that struck
the monolith down, but some strange charity
in the law of gravity, its force a want that binds us

to the earth, to streets we walk into many nations
of our city, each of us searching for one more
fragment of the palace, each bearing a separate prayer,
a separate music, level with one another as we speak.

III.

HEAVEN

In the bright crystal of your eyes
Show the havoc of fire, show its inspired works
And the paradise of its ashes. —PAUL ELUARD

The Island City of Dmitri Shostakovich

If my hands were cut off, I would continue to write music
with the pen between my teeth.   —DMITRI SHOSTAKOVICH

For months now I have crawled inside these preludes
and fugues, the color of night's icy structures
turning to water, polishing the silence.
There's a light sleeper just beneath the surface,
the sound in his head a threnody sweetening.
The very scent would melt a tyrant in his tomb.

Once Dmitri's desk drawer savored its privacies:
toy parodic marches full of spit and wobble,
a child's elegy, a Hebrew prayer. Stave after stave
tiny thorns and blossoms clustered on their stems.
It became his vital crime, this life, the drawer
drawn open like the jaw of a dreaming boy.

However stiff the vodka in his cup,
he felt the occasional season of tremors
tugging at his cheek, tightening the mask.
Those years you took a man to the toilet
to crack a joke, he said; you flushed the water to whisper
the gag, then laughed softly into your fist.

It's as if his body had a stranger in it,
an inmate huddled at the oven of his heart.
Come winter each boot print to his door
was a large ear filling up with snow.
Darkness too was white this time of year.
Dmitri slept with his bags packed beside him,

scared of the secret knock of police,
not that he would escape, only that he might
slip away in silence, the way sleet slips
into the Neva at night, without stirring
the uneasy peace of his wife, his children,
their sheets a quiet ruffle of wings.

City of islands, river fractured, charmed,
the brachia of its palace gates so shocked
with gleam they seemed suspended in the air.
Even St. Isaac's gilded cupola, emboldened
with the weight of its treasure, was one
cold burgeoning sun arrested in its flight.

And there, beside a northern bridge, the four horses
reared and grappling the sky before them
as if they would leap right out of their bronze—
the whole of it built on a swamp of human bones,
skeletons swept from the founding scaffolding
to light the crystal ceilings of the place.

However thick the cinder-block tenements,
factory smoke, curbsides heaped with soured snow,
however heavy the new Russia resting on its stilts,
a fabled frailty survived, each spired confection
plagued with cracks, weather-burnished, flood-prone,
the skies a frosty compress over a fevered gold.

You can hear them in the brooding momentum
of his bass, the patient rage and impacted stairwells,
a basement maze thrown open to the notes
that sketched his name: D-S-C-H: the brassy stretch
of a figure so long repressed it hungered
for refrain: D-S-C-H. That too had fever in it.

Such heat for a shivering sparrow of a man
skittish with fire and outstretched hands.
Such an enormous weight released he would have the dead
quaking in their sleep, rising to the final movement
as if it were their names buried in his.
Go there. Check the numbers on the headstones,

the bodiless effigies of friends gazing back.
There's a strength in the strings' lower reaches
that wears at this bitterness, a resolve
in the rock with the lily on its chest,
the sex of lime trees powdering the gravel,
their wind-bent spines bursting into song.

Passacaglia

Before wings, before the slightest desire
for wings, she thinks only of the ground
beneath her, there in the organ pedals,
the unsettled terrain she steps softly over,
slow at first, then slower, her feet shy

as giant misshapen hands, descending
toward some final boredom and release,
when having walked so far into solitude
she feels indistinguishable from the sound
she makes: she could play it in her sleep.

And so the variations as they spring up
through her calves, her torso, over her shoulders,
the clear veins that wrap around her wrists
and perish. She breaks into several bodies
conversing, swept up in the general spirit—

what the arm said, the incredulous ear,
the open question of her thighs, each rest
pulsing with the echo it consumes.
To be drawn to the cold of each new place,
passing through, the way a salamander slips

into ice-green water, shivering, precise,
the way a drop of morphine enters the blood.
It's as if a language, however blurred,
broke out of a language, a sweet strange
mourning in such long and tongueless throats.

As the bass swells the basilica shakes,
abandoned, save for the angels forever
blushed and thrown through a startle of ribbons,
clutching their tiny useless coronets.
Their fists are ripe and opulent as apples.

All as if they too had losses to bury
in the music, a thumb to discipline, a breath,
and what keeps them in their heaven is the same
skin skin imagines, what it recalls.
How winded they must be, befuddled, jinxed,

to bluster that way into silent horns,
their fingers aching. She feels them haloing
the loft like handsome and predatory birds.
Or falling, as angels will, through the feathered
flames in her hands, her legs. Light as ash.

Pilgrim

There's always a little bit of heaven in a disaster area.
—STAGE ANNOUNCEMENT AT WOODSTOCK

It is a day the sky throws down
a sting of sleet, when the movie
in my TV flickers with the fire

of its ecstatic children, the boy
at the traps who blurs his sticks,
looking up, his locks a drizzle

of good sweat and curls, the riffs
pouring down his arms, his toms,
a free hand flashing at the ride,

and me in the happy racket
where I watch, a shade envious
of those who felt on the brink

of a bluer June, charitable
as glass, who, caught in the crosshairs
of hope, tie-dye bull's-eyes

brightening their backs, in all
their bewildered self-permission,
took of the loaf as it passed their way

and buried their heads in the scent,
buried their trepidation: boom,
goes the mallet; it's what travels

deepest, the fist of bass
like a young heart or angry door,
a jet that drags its rumbling shield.

Small wonder, this cupped match,
the fingers' red glow, this pupil
like a solar eclipse; small wonder,

the sigh of hashish in the air,
that stifled cough and sweet affliction,
everywhere a ruinous traffic

of pilgrims in the mud: *no rain*,
no rain, they chant, and the sound of it
drowns in heaven's answer.

Even now I hear my own roof
crackle, one boy's rhythm thinning
out over the makeshift city

and its margins, here, so far
from the stage—to feel like a child
is never a child's feeling—far

from the smoke of someone else's war
thumping its enormous drum,
rain or no rain, scattering the birds.

Black Sun

So it was I came to a place
where the river slowed in its clay
and palsied oaks raised up their lace
of broken sky, bright with the cry

of enormous crows, the crowned
atmosphere under the crush
that noon sun brings, bearing down,
and I knew the white-winged thrash

of sleeplessness had to give in
to some greater danger, some dread
teetering forward like obsession
without focus, my body's bread

steaming in its shirt, the ghost
of what I held and why trailing off
behind me, until it was *my* ghost
out there, all my will to speak of,

save that which felt like another
working through me, a brother
will to move my legs, my shoulder,
whatever it took to make it over

the difficult time, which in time
would ease, no less inexplicable
than when it came, the smoky calm
of dusk darkening my table,

sharpening a star to pierce
the black mirror of the eye,
to still it, a flock of birds
high and dwindling, buried alive.

The Eyes of Odilon Redon

In a swoon and craggy spontaneity of sky,
the four horses of Apollo writhe, haunches
cumulus, limned in sparks,
lashed to the dazzled carrion of the sun.
It too writhes behind them, propagating light,
jeweling the coiled sea-worm below
which is terrible in size, though toothless,
blind, a lather of night-shade flecked with joy.

How far we've come from stretches
of nothing but black: when Odilon's firstborn
died of fever, sketch after sketch
laid sheets to the sickbed of empty hours,
his fingers charcoaled in the stuff
of spiders, severed heads, inscrutable grins,
buoyant, bereft. You would think Apollo's son
had crashed the chariot of daylight.

Where to put another saint radiant with arrows,
another watery cactus in the desert?
Call it what you will: melancholia's
origin is a gallery of heads, talking,
each with its gape of roots and losses somewhere
behind the canvas. Black, he said,
should be respected. Nothing prostitutes it.
Our gazes swell as if it were a little larger.

So too the thirst in each Cyclopic eye
he drew, fatted on ash and monastic weather,
each pupil without peer to calm
its pride, each head without body
to feed or suffer. Deprivation is a monocle,
a giant. The blinding of one eye
enflames its twin, inflates it into a bodiless
loneliness, impotent as monsters.

A teacher once told him to stare
long and hard at a chimney flue
until time would make it strange.
If your gaze remains, the dream will be alive.
Which is how the bits of coal
and disenchantment ignited in his sleep.
The patience of the true observer had fire in it.
His mood gave way to the dawning

crown of a second son, shocked with color,
to breech a cube of lighted toys.
Apollo's horses were no less figured,
crowned, galloping out a child's mind
with all the ferocity of a clear day.
Who wouldn't fatten on an infant gaze?
It vivified the wine's crystal, the sizzle
of meat, violets flapping open like an oven.

Do as nature does, he thought, create
sapphires, agates, precious metal, flesh.
Sun rolled its heavy head into his room,
across his canvas. Severed still—
it quickens the eye to see it—
though bristling with nerves, tendrils
everywhere, pulling worms
from the thrilled body of the world.

Joy

It is the sound of the great still bell
expectant as a bride, a thin bronze spider
drinking the porcelain at night.

It is the glint of the fly rubbing its hands
in the sun, the buzz of brilliant caterpillars
that carve the leaves of turnips and figs.

It leavens a melodious smoke, a largesse
of absence after a banquet, the empty glass
and its shiny circle, its halo of surprise.

It rises over the nerves of grass where they flicker,
the unspoken pleading of shirts on a line.
Go on and answer, chase it if you will.

It is the mouth open and asleep
welling up with the shush of surf,
the room refreshed in the rising water.

Terminal

Under an airport skylight drenched in rain,
I sat alone one night deep into endless
flight delays and cancellations, the same
announcer's weary news ghosting the place,

filling the throat of the empty concourse,
until there in the stretch of silence between
disappointments I heard another voice,
more fragile than hers, water-softened, thin,

taking on the flesh of where I waited,
a stranger beckoning, *you there, what you repress*
in your travels, no sooner glimpsed than faded,
buried in the shadowy moans of jets

afloat on their reflections, what you deny
at the hushed mouth of the terminal bar
thickening with smoke, under burning eyes
of the TV screens, one for departures,

the other arrivals, their lines resolving
to a timeless mantra, canceled, canceled,
what you sense in the shades of clouds dissolving
here where the wind and its continual

deferrals make an island of your table,
a troubled freedom of captivity
hour after hour, isn't this the middle
of your life, on the shores of a city

you're neither in nor out of, not quite,
these plate-glass walls at once a perfect picture
of chaos and stillness, of the quiet
dread that fills a room like a mirror

full of mirrors? Aren't these the lost letters
of future days, these waiting rooms of the dead
tired and unabashed, the old man leaning backwards,
on his face a page of news, discarded?

And there just ahead, do you feel it, can you,
as if the corridor were lit by a white
courtesy phone, the god you never knew
searching like a child from gate to gate?

Then I awoke, the ghost in me frightened
by a chill of numbers, no apology,
no grief, no music, and yet the lure of flights
circling above me, even as the sky

came down like a thing on fire, my head
dizzy with the rumors of beginnings
and endings, grapple and relief, of heart
valves fluttering their small incessant wings.

The Lovers of Rome

Say it's true, what the ceiling clouds imagine,
His apparition boiling out from a cluster
of angels wingless in their troubled flight,

writhing to keep His holy weight afloat.
As Adam relaxes, God pins His eye
on the gift of living just beyond His grasp.

We can never know the long nights that stained
the painter's brush, if he dreamt of boys
dipped in amber, a palette of the boldest

minerals and berries, and yes, time,
always more time on his back, more lamplight
hung in the scaffolding that held him.

What he conjured in his solitude—
the cadavers he opened like little mansions,
the figures he revived, those lovers of Rome

lifted high into the drying plaster—
they would stun the current of eyes below.
Such is the audacity of the place,

to perfect a lively stillness, the flames
of rock along the fluted colonnade,
flagstones strong as the floors of rivers.

Even the numinous scraps of fabric
blushing over the body's shame hover
with animal astonishment and stress.

There's something here on the cusp of waking
as if God's eye might open underneath us.
People walk softly and cough, leave their change.

They cannot exhaust the flesh they see.
Freakish, how art eats up the empty spaces,
these walls like skin so thoroughly tattooed,

needled by a hand at every anchor.
It's as if the room had swallowed the man
who in turn grew larger than the room.

So it is with any lover's image
watering the seams of the body it's in.
Say there is no other earth than this,

the ravenous dream of the dream-deprived.
God's mirror shines in the fountain of His garden.
Say we too look upward year after year,

that we wake odd hours on a chapel bench,
parched, sore and chosen, breathing dust: soon
the ripe fruit is falling through its shadow.

Blades of birdsong are whittling away the trees.
There's a comfort even in the voice
of temptation, singling us out, calling our name.

And what could be more tempting than to reply
in kind, to gather what a painter knows
of gardens and corpses, of the arcane

fibers gripping the bone, to bind them
into lives, his brush dividing light from dark?
If there is a self-portrait here, a secret

point of view, let it be the stray guardian
turning away, his face to the ceiling,
his fingers smeared in the cobalt of heaven.

He keeps plunging his hands back in
like birds at the busy ends of his arms.
How he longs to walk right through the plaster.

He keeps scouring his palms, or trying,
each over each like pieces of silver,
as if only the sky could rinse itself away.

If one man could bear such theater
above him, beaming down, such black bile
and broken sleep, if he suffered as much

under waves of fever, with the lust
that turns like a giant wheel of rain,
what you see is the best of him pushing back.

To perceive it takes a certain distance,
the way the figure in a mirror seems
more wholly conceived, more self-possessed

than the one we inhabit. Or stranger still,
how we slip skin to skin in the puzzle
of another's arms, taking shape there,

however shyly, as they too take shape.
Who wouldn't want to conceive a body,
not simply the bloodless shepherd of clouds

but something flush, polished, watched and cared for,
no less of the planet than marble or chalk.
Who would settle for mere flashes of hands

and legs, winged in shadows, our true faces
blind to themselves, our true backs trailing
a mystery behind us, anxious to be touched.

Heaven

I wake to the little fits of nails
and hammers going at it in the heat,
these roofers bent like Muslims

over their task, tacking down
the fiery ribwork of long metal slats,
so in time roofs too must carry

the sun on their backs, taking over
where the men leave off: go on,
say the hammers, a body can bear

just so much sky, so many large
and vacant hours of weather; go on,
sweet home, my wooden box of April,

you, the body that entombs
a body, that lowers its shoulder
into dry wind turning into snow,

you who palm our match light
from the draft which, come winter,
is stiff and bitter—nights moan

over the rock cliff like a man
in the fatal nonsense of his age—
while somewhere in the sheltering

future, however fugitive
or spare the lives there, under
the small-ribbed architecture

of sleep, I hear the fret
of tiny hammers; inside every
house, another, and so it goes,

into the dwarf eternities
of work and doors: going in:
going out: the chirping of the doors.

About the Author

Bruce Bond received a B.A. from Pomona College, an M.A. in English from Claremont Graduate School, and an M.A. in Music Performance from the Lamont School of Music. After working for many years as a classical and jazz guitarist, he went on to receive his Ph.D. in English from the University of Denver. His previous collections of poetry include *The Throats of Narcissus* (University of Arkansas Press, 2001), *Radiography* (Natalie Ornish Award, BOA Editions, 1997), *The Anteroom of Paradise* (Colladay Award, QRL, 1991), *Independence Days* (R. Gross Award, Woodley Press, 1990), and four chapbooks. His poetry has appeared in *The Yale Review, The Paris Review, The New Republic, The Threepenny Review, The Ohio Review, The Georgia Review,* and other journals, and he has received fellowships from the National Endowment for the Arts, the Texas Commission on the Arts, Bread Loaf Writer's Conference, Wesleyan Writers' Conference, MacDowell, Yaddo, and Sewanee Writers' Conference. Presently he is Professor of English at the University of North Texas and poetry editor for *American Literary Review.*